THE BATTLE OF THE ALAMO

Texans Under Siege

BY STEVEN OTFINOSKI

Consultant:
Richard Bell, PhD
Associate Professor of History
University of Maryland, College Park

CAPSTONE PRESS
a capstone imprint

Tangled History is published by Capstone Press,
1710 Roe Crest Drive, North Mankato, Minnesota 56003
www.mycapstone.com

Library of Congress Cataloging-in-Publication Data is available on the
Library of Congress website.

ISBN 978-1-5435-4198-4 (Hardcover)
ISBN 978-1-5435-4202-8 (Paperback)
ISBN 978-1-5435-4206-6 (eBook PDF)
ISBN 978-1-5435-4210-3 (Reflowable Epub)

Editorial Credits: Nick Healy, editor; Tracy McCabe, designer; Eric Gohl,
media researcher; Laura Manthe, production specialist

Photo Credits
Alamy: Chronicle, 76, The History Collection, 22, 42, The Picture Art
Collection, 33; Alan C. Huffines (Author) and Gary Zaboly (Illustrator),
"Blood of Noble Men: The Alamo Siege and Battle" (Eakin 1999): 50, 53;
Bridgeman Images: Private Collection/Wyeth, Newell Convers (1882–1945),
74; Capstone: 40; Getty Images: Bettmann, 48, Kean Collection, 38, 84;
Granger: 28, 57; iStockphoto: wynnter, 98; Library of Congress: 8, 15,
70, 101; North Wind Picture Archives: 66, 90; SuperStock: The Kobal
Collection (USA) Ltd, cover; Wikimedia: Public Domain, 4, 19, 60

Printed and bound in the United States of America.
PA49

TABLE OF CONTENTS

Stephen F. Austin

FOREWORD

In the Spanish family of American colonies, Texas was an unwanted relative. The most northern Spanish colony, Texas was a remote and rugged land. Although the area was first settled in the late 1600s, only 7,000 Spanish settlers were in Texas by 1793. The Comanche, the greatest warriors of the Southwest tribes, posed a serious threat to settlement. Despite these challenges, American settlers from the United States were beginning to move into Texas by the early 1800s. Then in 1821, Mexico won its independence from Spain.

The republic of Mexico, established in 1824, welcomed American settlers, called Texians. Mexico saw them as creating a buffer between Mexican provinces to the south and the Comanche to the north. To entice Americans to settle there, Mexico gave them land grants and told them they wouldn't have to pay taxes for at least seven years. Mexico even allowed the newcomers to bring along enslaved people they already owned, even though Mexico banned slavery in all its territories by 1829. Among the most prominent American colonist leaders, called empresarios, was 27-year-old Stephen Austin. He brought 300 families to settle on fertile land between the Colorado and Brazos Rivers in 1825. The Mexican government required all Texians to become Mexican citizens. Austin's colony and other Texians got along well with the Mexican government for almost a decade.

However, the Mexican government eventually became alarmed by the growing number of settlers from the United States. It also wasn't pleased with the number of enslaved people the Texians had with them—slaves who toiled for no pay and were treated harshly. In 1830, Mexico ended American immigration to Texas. Then in 1832, Antonio Lopez de Santa Anna became president of Mexico and the situation grew worse.

Santa Anna soon established a dictatorship in Mexico. Some Texians openly opposed Santa Anna, but Stephen Austin sought a peaceful compromise. He traveled to Mexico City in 1833 to meet with Santa Anna. The president refused to see him, and Austin was soon imprisoned.

When he was finally released a year and a half later, Austin returned to Texas, now committed to the cause of independence. In November 1835 the Texians organized a temporary government. Another transplanted American, Sam Houston, was named leader of the Texas military forces. Texians were joined in their fight by a number of Mexicans who also opposed Santa Anna, called Tejanos.

Concerned about this growing rebellion, Santa Anna sent his brother-in-law, Martin Perfect de Cós, north with an army in late 1835. Cós seized a Texian stronghold, the old provincial capital of San Antonio de Bexar, known today as the city of San Antonio, in south-central Texas. He also seized the old Spanish mission adjoining it called the Alamo. A Texian force, however, attacked and defeated him on December 11, 1835. Cós surrendered and was sent back to Mexico, promising that he would not return to Texas. When Santa Anna heard about the humiliating defeat of Cós, he was furious. He decided to lead an army north, retake San Antonio, and crush the rebels.

Back in San Antonio, many of the men who fought against Cós went home for Christmas with no thought of returning. Many of them believed the war with Mexico was over.

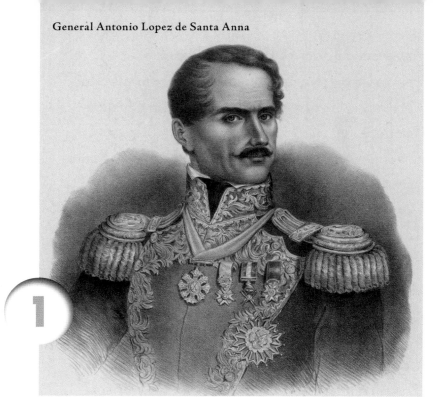

General Antonio Lopez de Santa Anna

1

"THE MEXICANS ARE UPON US"

General Santa Anna, in his bright red and black uniform, reined in his horse. He was surrounded by his dragoons, their armor gleaming in the winter sun. He looked down at the ribbon of blue below—the Rio Grande. For three weeks Santa Anna's army had trekked through the mountainous landscape of northern Mexico. Their trail was strewn with dead horses and oxen. Underfed and poorly clothed, dozens of soldiers had fallen ill and some had died. Others had deserted. But for Santa Anna these sacrifices were necessary. Once across the river, they would be in Texas, Mexico's northernmost province. Soon they would reach their final destination—the town of San Antonio de Bexar. Here they would confront the rebels who held the town and destroy them. The Texians would not expect his army to arrive in the dead of winter, giving Santa Anna the element of surprise. Rising up in his saddle, Santa Anna drew his shining sword. He waved it in the air and his soldiers began to cross the ice cold river.

Jim Bowie

The Alamo, San Antonio
February 21, 1836, 2:00 p.m.

Colonel Bowie looked on approvingly as several men worked on fortifying a wall of the Alamo. The walls were thick and tall but had no openings through which a gun could be fired. They also had no protected platforms where men could fire from behind the walls. And a gap in the southeast corner of the Alamo's walls measured 50 yards (43 meters) wide. There was work to do.

At age 40, Jim Bowie was an American legend. He was known for his deadly skill with the big knife that still bears his name—the Bowie knife. Bowie had arrived in Texas in 1828 and two years later became a Mexican citizen. He married the daughter of the vice governor of the province and became a wealthy landowner. Then tragedy struck.

In 1833 his wife, two children, and father-in-law died in a cholera epidemic. Bowie's loyalties began to shift from Mexico to the Texians and Tejanos calling for independence. He became a colonel in the volunteer army led by Sam Houston. Houston had sent Bowie to San Antonio a month earlier.

The Alamo was a sprawling compound more than three acres (1.2 hectares) in size. At the center of the old Spanish mission was a rectangular plaza of bare ground the size of a city block. On the plaza's south side was a long one-story building and the main entrance. On the east side was a long two-story building used as barracks and next to it a corral. In an open gap between the east and south sides stood the Alamo church, a thick-walled ruin. The west side faced the town, about 400 yards (365 m) away. Both the west and north sides were bordered by 12-foot (4-m) walls.

Houston saw the Alamo as indefensible. He wanted Bowie to destroy it and abandon San Antonio. But upon his arrival, Bowie quickly changed his mind. He was impressed with what commander Colonel James Neill had done to build up the Alamo's defenses. "The salvation of Texas depends in great measure in keeping Bejar [Bexar] out of the hands of the enemy," he wrote in a letter to Texas governor Henry Smith.

Neill had departed the Alamo to go home to visit his sick wife and children. He left 27-year-old William Barrett Travis, a leader in the independence movement, in charge. But the men resisted Travis's leadership. They preferred Bowie's easy ways to Travis's strict military discipline. The two men struck a compromise. Travis would be in charge of the regular army soldiers. Bowie would command the volunteer troops, which were growing in number.

As the men finished their work, Bowie felt a wave of nausea pass over him. He gritted his teeth until it passed. He had been feeling ill for several days now and hoped whatever he had would run its course. As a war with was Mexico underway, this was no time for him to be sick.

William Travis

Colonel William Travis finished his letter, put down his pen, and looked out at the setting sun. He had written many letters in the past several weeks. They included letters to the governor and to Sam Houston. This one was addressed to Colonel James Fannin at Goliad, 80 miles (129 kilometers) to the southeast. All Travis's letters had a common message—send reinforcements.

Like many of the Alamo defenders, Travis had come to Texas to start a new life. He hailed from Alabama, where he had taught school and then become a lawyer. He departed in 1831, leaving behind a pregnant wife and son. He kept his reasons for leaving Alabama to himself. In Texas he became a spokesman for independence, but he didn't believe in independence for all people. He had been a slaveholder in Alabama, and in Texas he bought a new slave. The enslaved man was named Joe, and through no choice of his own, he would end up at the Alamo.

Travis saw in the struggle with Mexico a chance to achieve fame and glory. Bowie was a good man, but Travis rankled at sharing command of the Alamo with him. He put down his pen and folded the letter. He would wait until morning to send it off with a scout to Goliad. He didn't want anyone to miss the party the men were throwing tonight. It was in celebration of George Washington's birthday. Travis decided the men needed a chance to blow off some steam after all their work on the fort. Maybe he did too.

Davy Crockett

Main Plaza, San Antonio
February 22, 7:30 p.m.

"Where's your fiddle, Davy?" several men cried. "We need some music."

Davy Crockett grinned and set off immediately for the stone house in the plaza, where he was staying. He didn't need any persuading to play his fiddle. Or to tell a tall tale about himself. Or to give

Davy Crockett's days as an American frontiersman grew into legend.

a rousing speech. At age 49, Crockett was a national celebrity, even a greater one than Bowie. He was a frontiersman known for killing bears and fighting American Indians. More recently, he had served two terms in the U.S. Congress from his native state of Tennessee. But Crockett lost his seat in the 1833 election. He left Washington, D.C., saying, "You may all go to Hell and I will go to Texas." He got there in the fall of 1835. He had arrived at the Alamo only recently with 12 followers from Tennessee, all sharpshooters. He wanted to help the Texian cause, but he also saw opportunity for himself. If Texas became free and joined the United States, he could return to politics as a governor or senator.

Fiddle in hand, Crockett came back to the plaza and perched himself on a low wall. John McGregor, a red-haired Scotsman, was tuning up his bagpipes. "Hey, Davy," McGregor cried, "let's see who can make the most noise."

Davy grinned. "That's one contest you're not going to win, John," he said. Then he began to play a lively tune as the men and women of San Antonio danced to the music.

William Travis

Travis was awakened from a sound sleep by the sound of excited voices and the creaking of cart wheels. He rushed outside to see what the commotion was about. Whole families of Tejanos were leaving town, on foot and in carts filled with their belongings. He asked several men where they were going but got no answers. Finally, a Tejano he was friendly with told him the stunning news: "Santa Anna is coming!"

It couldn't be true, Travis told himself. While the Mexican general might be planning an assault, surely he wouldn't attempt it in the depths of winter. But Travis had to be certain the rumors were false. Together with Dr. John Sutherland, he rushed to the San Fernando church, whose tower was the highest point in San Antonio. From the tower they scanned the horizon to the west and south. They saw nothing. But, cautious as always, Travis left a soldier to stand sentry in the tower.

"If you see soldiers approaching, sound the bell at once," Travis told the sentry. Then he returned to his headquarters. Dr. Sutherland went to the general store to help owner Nat Lewis go over his inventory of supplies.

Susanna Dickinson

The stone house, Main Plaza
February 23, 11:00 a.m.

"Hush, Angelina," Susanna Dickinson said to her young daughter, who was playing with a doll. She didn't want her to wake up the men in the house. Her husband, Almeron, and Colonel Crockett were already up and about. But most of Crockett's Tennessee riflemen were still sleeping after their late night. Susanna felt they had earned their rest. She didn't mind sharing their residence with the Tennesseans. After all, they were paying her to wash their clothes, providing the family with some much-needed income. Also, she enjoyed the company of these stalwart men and especially their leader, Colonel Crockett. She loved to listen to the stories of his adventures.

Susanna Dickinson

Like him, she was a native of Tennessee. It was there, at age 15, she'd met and married Almeron, a blacksmith. Two years later, the couple settled in the Texas town of Gonzales. Almeron later joined the Texian fighting force and left to fight at the Battle of Bexar. Susanna and Angelina had stayed behind in Gonzales, 69 miles (111 km) to the west. Then looters broke into their home, and she fled to San Antonio and joined her husband.

Dickinson had seen the locals leaving the town that morning. She was worried that the Mexicans may be coming. However, she had faith in her husband and in Davy Crockett and Jim Bowie. They would hold the enemy back, at least until reinforcements arrived. Surely more men would come to save the Alamo.

John Sutherland

Just outside San Antonio
February 23, 1:30 p.m.

Dr. Sutherland was as perplexed as Travis. At 1 p.m. the sentry had rung the tower bell. They rushed to the church, but when they looked they could see nothing. Another false alarm. Sutherland offered to ride out to see if there was any truth to the sentry's sighting. "If we see anything, we will come back riding hard," he told Travis. Volunteer John Smith, who knew the country well, agreed to ride with Sutherland. The two men left at once.

At age 42, Sutherland was a widower from Virginia and one of two doctors at the Alamo. He assisted the other more experienced physician, Dr. Pollard.

The two horsemen rode up a small slope about a mile and a half from town. From the summit they looked down and saw a terrible sight. Hundreds of Mexican cavalrymen were below, heading in their direction. Sutherland and Smith quickly turned their horses around and set out for town. The ground was slick from rain, and Sutherland's horse slipped. The animal pitched Sutherland forward into the air. Sutherland fell to the ground and the horse landed on his legs. Smith helped him back into the saddle, and they were off again. As they raced to San Antonio they could hear the loud peal of the church bell sounding the warning.

Gregorio Esparza

North Flores Street, San Antonio
February 23, 1:45 p.m.

Gregorio Esparza was surprised to see his good friend John Smith ride up to his front door, out of breath and excited. Smith told him the shocking news that Santa Anna and his army were on their way. Esparza, a loyal Tejano, had fought at the Battle of Bexar. But he had not intended to fight for the

Gregorio Esparza

Alamo again. He was going to take his wife and four children away from San Antonio to a safer place. But now Esparza realized it was too late to get out of town before the soldiers arrived.

"Well," he told his wife, "I'm going to the fort."

Ana Esparza showed little surprise at her husband's decision. "Well, if you go, I'm going along, and the whole family," she replied. And with that they packed up what belongings they could and headed for the footbridge that would take them to the Alamo.

William Travis

Travis had just finished another note to Colonel Fannin when Sutherland came hobbling into the room supported by Davy Crockett. The doctor explained how he had fallen off his horse. Travis told him to get into the Alamo at once. But Sutherland would hear none of it. He argued that he was in no shape to help defend the fort. He would be put to better use as a rider, going out to seek reinforcements. Travis reluctantly agreed. He already had a scout picked to take the letter to Goliad, but gave Sutherland another letter to carry to Gonzales to ask for help. It read: "The enemy in large force is in sight. We want men and provisions. Send them to us. We have 150 men and are determined to defend the Alamo to the last. Give us assistance."

Sutherland left with John Smith again by his side.

Davy Crockett

As Sutherland left, Crockett was also feeling in need of a duty in protecting the fort. "Colonel," he said to Travis, "here am I. Assign me to a position, and I and my twelve boys will try and defend it."

With little hesitation Travis assigned Crockett and his riflemen to the palisade erected on the south side of the Alamo. This was the weakest spot in the fort's defense. If anyone could hold off the enemy in this vulnerable place, it was Crockett and his sharpshooters. Crockett straightened the coonskin cap on his head and was out the door.

John Sutherland

Sutherland and Smith got out of town with little trouble. The Mexican troops were still marching in and paying no attention to who was coming and leaving San Antonio. As they looked back at the town, they were astonished to see storekeeper Nat Lewis running toward them. He carried heavy saddlebags on his shoulders.

"Why aren't you staying?" Sutherland asked him.

"I am not a fighting man," replied Lewis. "I'm a businessman."

As they rode off, Sutherland, a fighting man, felt the fight had been knocked out of him. Suddenly the pain in his leg seemed unbearable. He thought about turning back to town, but then heard the crack of a cannon. It was too late. The battle had started. He spurred on his horse to catch up with Smith.

Susanna Dickinson

The stone house
February 23, 2:45 p.m.

Dickinson was surprised to see her husband gallop up to their house in the plaza. "The Mexicans are upon us," he cried. "Give me the babe, and jump up behind me." She handed Angelina up to him and then climbed up on the horse. Without another word to her, Almeron Dickinson rode straight to the Alamo.

Santa Anna

The general stood atop the tower of the San Fernando church and looked out. Below him the plaza was filled with his soldiers, hundreds of them. A mere 80 yards (73 m) away the Texians were holed up in the Alamo. There was little point in mounting a major assault until more of his troops arrived. They would bring heavier artillery to break down the walls of the old mission. Santa Anna would wait. In the past hour, both Jim Bowie and Travis had sent messengers out to meet him. They wanted to see if they could negotiate a peaceful surrender, in which he would guarantee the safety of their men. But Santa Anna would give no such guarantee. He ordered men to raise a blood red flag up the flagpole. Its message was clear: Surrender or no quarter and mercy will be given once the fighting starts.

William Travis

The Alamo
February 23, 3:30 p.m.

Travis's heart sank when he saw the red flag snapping in the breeze. But he knew that surrender could also mean death. Santa Anna was not to be trusted. Wasn't it better to die as men, defending the Alamo, than to go peacefully to slaughter? In that moment, Travis realized this was the moment he had been waiting for all his life, a moment of honor and glory. He turned to the men arming the 18-pound cannon, the largest piece of artillery in the Alamo. The cannon could fire an 18-pound cannonball at distant targets.

"Gentlemen," he said, "prepare to fire."

The cannon boomed its message of defiance. The battle had begun.

2

Jim Bowie

"DO NOT BE AFRAID"

Jim Bowie

Jim Bowie woke with a chill in his bones. He had collapsed the night before and now knew that he was seriously ill. Dr. Pollard had been unable to determine what the mysterious ailment was that had settled in his chest. Bowie made the difficult decision to step down from his command. He sent word to Travis that he would be sole commander of the Alamo. Now Bowie had another difficult decision to make. He feared his illness would spread to others if he stayed in the barracks. Therefore, he ordered two men to carry his pallet to a small room near the main gate. He was most concerned about quarantining himself from his sister-in-law, Juana, and her sister Gertrudis. They were the only members of his family left.

Before the men moved him, he called Juana to his side. He took her hand and said, "Sister, do not be afraid. I leave you with Colonel Travis, Colonel Crockett, and other friends. They are gentleman and will treat you kindly."

Tears came to Juana's eyes as he ordered the men to carry him out. As they moved him to his new room he wondered if we would ever see Juana again.

William Travis

His headquarters, the Alamo
February 24, 7:30 p.m.

It had been a long day, the first day of the siege of the Alamo. Surrounded by the enemy, the defenders of the Alamo had no way to get food and supplies from the outside and they had withstood constant bombardment. Travis had visited his men on the parapets, continually encouraging them to return gunfire with the Mexicans. It felt good to be in command, and he was grateful to Bowie for stepping down. But Travis also felt regret. Bowie's spirit, courage, and leadership would be missed.

Santa Anna had kept up the artillery fire all day. Now with nightfall he was waging what Travis considered psychological warfare—tactics meant to wear down the will of the defenders. The men could hear Santa Anna's military bands playing loudly. Bugles blared and drums pounded in the night air. It put the men on edge and deprived them of the rest they needed for the coming day.

As tired as he was, Travis sat down at his desk to write another appeal. This letter would be sent to Gonzales, where he hoped Gail Borden, publisher of the local newspaper, would print it. It was as frank and straightforward as Travis could make it.

Fellow citizens and compatriots—

I am besieged, by a thousand or more of the Mexicans under Santa Anna—I have sustained a continual Bombardment & cannonade for 24 hours & and have not lost a man . . . . I call on you in the name of Liberty, of patriotism & everything dear to the American character, to come to our aid, with all dispatch . . . . If this call is neglected, I am determined to sustain myself as long as possible & die like a soldier who never forgets what is due to his own honor & that of his country—
VICTORY OR DEATH

William Barret Travis

Lt. Col. Comdt.

Santa Anna

Santa Anna was determined not to be idle while awaiting the arrival of more soldiers. Two new batteries had been set up the previous night within striking distance of the Alamo's entrance. The general gave the order to fire. At the same time, General Castrillon led a battalion of 300 men to within 100 yards (91 m) of the fort. They opened fire on the vulnerable southern wall where Crockett's sharpshooters were stationed and returned the fire. The battle there lasted two hours. Then Santa Anna ordered a full retreat. The casualty list included two dead soldiers and six wounded. Santa Anna had a new respect for the rebels' marksmanship. If he was to overtake the Alamo, he saw that it would take a greater force. More troops and artillery were on the way. He would wait.

James Fannin

Colonel Fannin reread the latest message from the Alamo. There was a note of desperation in it that Travis's earlier letters didn't have. Fannin considered himself a good soldier. He had come to Texas from his native Georgia to buy

James Fannin

land and trade slaves. But when the question of independence for Texas arose, he fully supported it. Now he was assigned to defend Goliad. He and the 450 men under him had built a palisade they proudly named Fort Defiance.

But the time had come to answer the call for help from the Alamo, which lay 80 miles (129 km) to the north. It would take them days to get there. Fannin gave the command to move out. The men and supply wagons, pulled by oxen, moved down a hill to the San Antonio River. They had gotten only 200 yards (183 m) when one of the wagons broke down. No sooner was it repaired than two more wagons broke down. They used the oxen to drag the four cannons in the wagons across the river. By the time they reached the other side with all the artillery, the sun was setting. Fannin could see that the men were exhausted and led them back to the fort to sleep. They would get an early start in the morning for San Antonio.

Davy Crockett

The Alamo's southern wall
February 26, 4:30 p.m.

Crockett was proud of his Tennessee riflemen. They had held the enemy back for two days and showed no sign of tiring. Each man kept four or five long rifles by his side on the parapet, ready to fire.

Their leader was at his post, kneeling down behind the low wall, when he saw something. In the distance, a Mexican stood in the open as he built an earthwork. Crockett laid down and rested his rifle on the edge of the parapet. He got the Mexican in his sights, cocked the trigger, and fired. The man at the earthwork fell down and lay still. Crockett's bullet had found its mark.

Crockett stood up to reload his rifle. He was willing to risk getting shot by the enemy. He figured their antiquated muskets couldn't shoot that far. They would have to get a lot closer to bring down Davy Crockett. And he was determined to see that they didn't get that close.

Susanna Dickinson

The Alamo's kitchen
February 26, 5 p.m.

Susanna Dickinson finished shaping the ground corn into small cakes and put them in the oven. It was nearly time for dinner. She and the other women worked feverishly to get the meal ready. Feeding more than 200 people—men, women, and children—each day was no easy task. But Dickinson liked being busy. It kept her mind off the siege. When she wasn't in the kitchen cooking or doing laundry for Crockett and his men, Dickinson was assisting Dr. Pollard. More than 30 people were sick or injured and needed medical care. Medical supplies were scarce, but the doctor did what he could to make his patients comfortable. In the few free moments she had, Dickinson would rush up the platform at the church. She would visit her husband, who was manning the artillery there. She enjoyed talking to the other men working with him. Each one had his own story to tell of how he came to Texas.

Ana Esparza, Gregorio's wife, came into the kitchen to ask if the corn cakes were ready. Dickinson opened the hot oven, took out the tray of baked cakes, and prepared another batch. The men had healthy appetites and needed plenty of corn cakes. Dickinson tried not to think about the day when the corn—and the beef—would run out at the Alamo. What would they do for food then?

James Fannin

It had been a rough morning for the men of Fort Defiance. They awoke to find the oxen had wandered off. The men assigned to tether them hadn't done their job. By the time the oxen were rounded up, the men were divided about what to do next. Fannin agreed to have a council meeting by the riverbank. Many of the volunteers felt it was foolhardy to continue the expedition. They pointed out that they were low on food supplies and ammunition. They argued their first duty was to defend Goliad, not abandon it. Fannin listened carefully to everything that was said. He felt that the arguments put forth for not going were reasonable ones. He agreed to return to the fort. Later that afternoon he wrote a letter to acting governor James Robinson. "It was deemed expedient to return to this post and complete the fortifications," he wrote. Fannin didn't rule out going to Travis's aid, but not right now.

The Spanish built the Alamo near the San Antonio River in the early 1700s. The fortress first served as a Roman Catholic mission.

"HOLD OUT!"

Santa Anna

San Antonio
February 28, 10:20 a.m.

Santa Anna was growing impatient. The siege was in its sixth day and a majority of his troops had not yet arrived. He was most disappointed in the

delay of General Antonio Gaona, who was leading a thousand men. Santa Anna was also worried that Colonel Fannin was on his way to the Alamo with 400 Texians. Their arrival could complicate the struggle and delay a Mexican victory. But he would bide his time. Meanwhile, he would do all in his power to discourage the rebels inside the Alamo. To that end, he ordered a new artillery attack on the fort.

James Fannin

Fort Defiance, Goliad
February 29, 1 p.m.

Colonel Fannin listened politely to messenger James Bonham, who had just arrived from the Alamo. Bonham was trying to convince him to start out again for the fort. Fannin was reluctant to do so. His volunteers had little

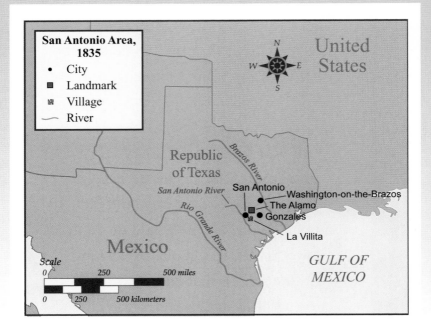

interest in making the dangerous trek. Besides that, news had arrived that Mexican troops had attacked and nearly wiped out the Texian town of San Patrico, about 50 miles (80 km) to the south. His instincts told him to stay put and be prepared to defend Goliad from a similar attack.

"I'm sorry," he told Bonham, "but we've got to stay here and defend our own people."

"Then you won't come to help Travis?" replied Bonham.

"No," said Fannin. "And I advise you not to return

to the Alamo. Only certain death awaits you there."

Bonham looked at the colonel, his eyes growing cold. He spit on the ground.

"Nothing can stop me from going back," he said. "And I think you should send a reply. You owe Travis at least that."

Fannin could think of nothing to say. And with that, Bonham rushed out the door.

William Travis

Alamo headquarters
March 1, 3 a.m.

It was the middle of the night and yet Travis was unable to sleep. After six days of bombardment he was beginning to lose hope. Although the food supplies were still ample, ammunition and gunpowder were running low. He had ordered the men not to fire their guns except to repel a direct attack. They needed reinforcements—badly.

Suddenly the stillness was broken by a sentry's cry.

"Riders!" he shouted.

Travis ran to the wall. "Friend or foe?" he cried to the sentry.

William Travis

"Can't tell yet," was the reply.

The night was black and they could only hear the pounding of horses' hooves on the hard earth. Before Travis could give the order to hold fire, a nervous rifleman fired a shot into the darkness. A man's voice came out of the night, crying loudly that he had been hit. The man spoke English. These were friends!

Travis ordered the gate to be opened and the men rode into the main plaza. John Smith was with the riders and immediately reported to Travis.

"I bring 32 volunteers from Gonzales, Colonel," he said.

Travis embraced his scout. Reinforcements at last!

Dr. Pollard was tending to the rider who had been hit in the foot by the sentry's bullet.

The rest of the company was warmly welcomed by the Alamo men. Could Fannin's 400 men be far behind? Travis wondered. He was feeling so hopeful that he decided when dawn came that he would allow the men to fire freely back at the enemy's fire.

Sam Houston

Washington-on-the Brazos, Texas
March 1, 3 p.m.

Among the 41 delegates to the Texas convention, Sam Houston stood out. He wore buckskin breeches and a bright red flannel cloth with a hole cut out for his head. While other delegates shivered and complained about the cold in the unheated building, Houston showed no signs of displeasure.

He was a strong advocate for a declaration of independence, which these men were here to create. A committee of five was busy writing the document. The declaration of independence would give Houston the power he sought to lead an army of volunteers and regular soldiers to fight the Mexicans. Their first destination, he vowed to himself, would be the Alamo.

Jim Bowie

His room in the Alamo
March 2, 2:15 p.m.

Jim Bowie was a man of action, but now he was hopelessly out of the action. His mysterious illness had only gotten worse since the siege had begun. At times, he hardly had the strength to sit up on his pallet. But while his body was weak, his spirit remained strong. When he felt strong enough, he had several men lift him on a litter and carry him on the stretcher to the plaza to speak with the other defenders. He reminded them that Travis was in charge and needed to be obeyed. He urged them to keep fighting and to not give up hope.

This afternoon he called his men again to carry him from his room. This time they took him to the rooms where Juana and Gertrudis were staying. As soon as Juana saw him, her pale face brightened. Both she and her sister embraced him. They sat and he lay on his litter and talked. He told them how excited he was about the volunteers who had arrived from Gonzales. He assured the women that more help would soon be coming. In his heart he wasn't certain this was true. But he kept his doubts to himself.

William Travis

Alamo headquarters
March 2, 5 p.m.

The hope of more reinforcements was beginning to dim for Travis. It had been several days since news of Fannin's march came and he had still not arrived. But Travis knew that his men would fight to the last man if it came to that. He silently prayed that it would not come to that.

Suddenly he could hear a great commotion outside his door. Something was happening in the town. He ran to the wall where Crockett and others stood, rifles at the ready. They listened to the sound of hundreds of men shouting. The men were chanting "Santa Anna! Santa Anna!" over and over.

"It looks like the general got himself some reinforcements, too," said Crockett dryly.

Travis shook his head. From the sound of it, Santa Anna's army was now complete.

Santa Anna

Military Plaza, San Antonio
March 2, 5:10 p.m.

Santa Anna gazed with a great sense of satisfaction at the more than 1,000 new troops. General Gaona had arrived at last and not a moment too soon. Santa Anna's army now stood at 2,400 soldiers, including infantry and cavalry units. Better yet, news had just arrived of General Urrea's victory at San Patricio. And there was no sign that Colonel Fannin was coming from Goliad. As Santa Anna inspected his new troops he decided the time to strike had come. The general gave the command to ring the bells of the San Fernando church. It would sound the doom of the men of the Alamo.

William Travis

The Alamo
March 3, 11 a.m.

Travis was talking to some men when the sentries cried that a lone rider was coming. It was the ever-loyal James Bonham. A skilled horseman, Bonham managed to ride fast enough to elude the Mexicans surrounding the fort. The gate opened and Bonham rode in. A crowd of men gathered around him as he dismounted his horse. No one was happier to see him than Travis.

Bonham brought both bad and good news. The bad news was that Fannin would not be coming to their aid. The good news was contained in a letter from Major Robert Williamson at Gonzales.

"Tonight we await some 300 reinforcements from Washington, Bastrop, Brazoria, and San Felipe and no time will be lost in providing you assistance," Williamson wrote. In a postscript he added, "For God's sake hold out until we can assist you."

Travis vowed that they would do so.

Sam Houston was a soldier and served as governor of Tennessee before he moved to Texas, where he became a leader in the effort to gain independence from Mexico.

Sam Houston

It was official. The committee of five had presented a declaration of Texas independence the day before and now every delegate, including Houston, signed it. Five copies of the declaration would be sent to key communities, including Bexar. Houston was confident that Fannin and his men were on the way to the Alamo. He also believed, from Travis's last message, that the defenders could hold out until reinforcements arrived.

Leaving the drafty building where they had accomplished so much, Houston joined his fellow Texians for a well-earned celebration. After that, he too would head for the Alamo.

"VICTORY OR DEATH!"

Mexican soldiers sent a message to those inside the Alamo's walls by raising a red flag on San Fernando church in San Antonio.

William Travis

It had been another long day of bombardment, and Travis was bone tired. But he was not too tired to sit down and write. Writing to the outside world for help was a way to keep hope alive. But time, he well knew, was running out.

"A blood red banner waves from the church of Bexar, and in the camp above us, in token that the war is one of vengeance against rebels," he wrote to the president at Washington-on-the-Brazos. After pleading once more for men and supplies, he ended his letter with the words "God and Texas!—Victory or Death!"

Among the other letters Travis wrote by the flickering light of his candle was one to David Ayers. Ayers was temporarily caring for Travis's son Charles. "Take care of my little boy," Travis wrote. "If the country should be saved, I may make for him a splendid fortune; but if the country be lost and I should perish, he will have nothing but the proud recollection that he is the son of a man who died for his country."

Travis put the letters in a packet and stalked out into the plaza. His good friend Joseph Smith was waiting for him. Smith took the packet and mounted his horse. A group of men went outside the Alamo's walls to draw fire from the Mexican infantry. The diversion allowed Smith to ride safely past the Mexican batteries. Convinced Smith had gotten out safely, Travis returned to his rooms to try to get some rest.

Santa Anna

San Antonio
March 4, 9:10 a.m.

The booming of the big cannon was sweet music to the general's ears. Shot after shot pounded the weakened walls of the Alamo. While the artillery men were kept busy, however, most of the Mexican troops were inactive. They would need to rest,

Mexican soldiers dug trenches to move their cannons closer to the Alamo's walls.

Santa Anna decided, to save their strength for the final assault. But he alone would not make the decision about when to make that assault. He would hold a conference with his senior officers that very afternoon. It was unlike him to bring others into the decision-making process. But he felt by doing so he would help unify his men as they moved forward to victory.

Davy Crockett

Crockett's sunny disposition was beginning to fail him. As he talked to his Tennessee riflemen during a lull in the fighting, his words were deadly serious. "I think we ought to march out and die in the open air," he told them. "I don't like to be hemmed up." The men nodded in agreement. They too were willing to fight and die, if it came to that. But they wanted to be free of the walls surrounding them. Just then another cannonball struck the wall. Crockett gripped his rifle and returned to the fight.

Manuel Fernandez Castrillon

Santa Anna's headquarters, San Antonio
March 4, 4 p.m.

Once again, General Castrillon found himself at odds with his leader. In his conference with his officers, Santa Anna called for an assault on the Alamo in two days. Most of the others agreed.

Castrillon, General Cós, and a few others did not. They argued that they should wait for the arrival of heavier cannons to knock down the Alamo's walls.

There was another issue that Castrillon and Santa Anna did not see eye to eye on. It was the treatment of any prisoners taken in the final fight. Castrillon felt that they should be shown mercy as captives. He spoke of "principles regarding the rights of men, philosophical and humane principles which did them honor." Santa Anna brushed his argument aside. He said that any rebels who were not killed outright would be executed. It was, he said, what traitors deserved. Then he brought the long meeting to an end with nothing resolved. He would reach a final decision on the time of the attack himself after all.

Castrillon walked out of the headquarters of the general and into the gathering darkness. He looked up at the first glittering stars in the night sky and wondered what the next day would bring. He had hoped to be a mediating force in this campaign. Yet so far his efforts were fruitless. Once again, he saw himself as the "hard-luck general."

Santa Anna

Santa Anna closely examined the Mexican woman who stood before him. She had fled the Alamo and had asked to see him. Was she sent by Travis to see if the general would consider a peaceful surrender? Or was she really opposed to the rebels' cause? Santa Anna wasn't sure. He would listen to what she had to say and then decide. The woman explained that the men were discouraged and tired and their supplies and ammunition were running low. The general nodded, said little, and dismissed her. But he saw no reason to doubt her assessment. The time was ripe for attack. He decided to disregard Castrillon's call to wait. They would attack before dawn on Sunday, March 6.

William Travis gathered the men inside the Alamo and asked them to choose whether they would stay and fight or flee to safety.

William Travis

Main plaza, the Alamo
March 5, 5 p.m.

With a lull in the fighting, Travis decided the moment was right for an assembly. Time was growing short and the men had to know what they were up against. As word spread about the meeting, the plaza filled up with men. Even poor Jim Bowie, sicker than ever, was there. His faithful followers had carried him in his litter to the plaza. Mrs. Dickinson, whose husband stood with the other gunners, lingered in the back. She looked as anxious as anyone to hear what Travis had to say.

Travis cleared his throat, looked around at the anxious faces, and began to speak. "I won't pretend that our situation isn't bleak," he began. "There is little hope reinforcements will arrive to help us now. Our only choices remain to surrender, attempt to escape, or stay and fight. I have made my decision to stay and fight. Now it is up to each of you to decide what you will do. I urge you to stay here and fight to the end. But I will not judge any man who decides to do otherwise. If you want to leave, I ask you to step forward now."

Louis Rose

Main plaza, the Alamo
March 5, 5:15 p.m.

Louis Rose did not consider himself a coward. He had been a soldier for much of his 50 years and fought with the French Emperor Napoleon in Russia. He had come to Texas in 1826 and worked as a log cutter. He came to San Antonio in December of the previous year and fought against General Cós. He stayed on when other men left to go home. Rose never married and had no family. No one would mourn him if he died at the Alamo. And yet the battle for Texas' independence was not really his battle. He still considered himself first and last a Frenchman.

And so when Travis made his offer, Rose stepped forward. He had hoped that a few others would do the same, but no one else moved. They were all staying. Travis looked him in the eye, not unkindly, and nodded.

"This meeting is over," he said.

Martin Perfecto de Cós

San Antonio
March 5, 6 p.m.

General de Cós had his orders. In the early morning hours, he was to advance his column and pause 200 yards (183 m) north of the Alamo. There he was to wait for the command to attack. He now went about inspecting his men and their muskets.

General Martin Perfecto de Cós

He made sure that their bayonets were sharpened and fixed to their firearms. The guns would be used in the initial attack, but they would be of little use in close combat. Any men who made it inside the fort would be stabbing the enemy with their bayonets. He wondered how many of his men would make it that far. He knew from experience that the Texians would not give up without a fight. Cós also knew that his brother-in-law, Santa Anna, would be watching him.

The general would expect him to redeem himself after his defeat at the Alamo last December. Cós was determined not to disappoint him.

Gregorio Esparza

The Alamo
March 5, 8 p.m.

It was quiet, too quiet, outside the walls of the Alamo, Gregorio Esparza decided. It seemed like the calm before the storm. The Mexicans were up to something, though no one knew exactly what. The other gunners were talking with Almeron Dickinson and his wife. They were trying to take their minds off what the morning might bring. But Gregorio didn't join them. It wasn't because he felt left out as a Tejanos. He felt closer to some of the Texians than his own brothers, who had enlisted in Santa Anna's army. No, the reason he wandered away was because there was someone else's company he craved. He went to the building where his wife stayed. The children were asleep already. He held a finger to his lips, a signal for her not to awaken them. Then he lay down by her side and talked softly. They whispered to each other in the dark for a time and then went to sleep in each other's arms.

Louis Rose

The walls of the Alamo
March 5, 8:10 p.m.

Rose packed his few belongings into a bag and waited for night to fall. Only then would it be safe for him to leave the Alamo. After the meeting, he talked with the two men he most respected—Jim Bowie and Davy Crockett. Bowie tried to convince him to stay. Crockett felt he wouldn't make it to a Texian town alive. Both men, however, agreed that this was not his fight and there was no dishonor in his leaving. He thought his chances of getting away were good. His skin was dark and he spoke Spanish. Any guards he passed would take him for a Mexican. Taking a deep breath, Rose climbed over the low wall of the cattle pen. Then he struck out for the San Antonio River. He did not look back.

Susanna Dickinson

The Alamo chapel
March 5, 10 p.m.

Dickinson tried to get her daughter to settle down and go to sleep, but it was impossible. The other children in the chapel were awake and talking and Angelina wouldn't be separated from them. Suddenly the door of the chapel opened and Colonel Travis entered. She was amazed at how calm and quiet he seemed. Travis went around the room and spoke to each child in a gentle voice. When he stood before Angelina he ran his hand across her blond hair and smiled. Dickinson wondered if her daughter made him think of his own girl, born after he left his wife. Then she remembered he had never seen her.

"I want to give you something, dear," Travis said softly. He removed a gold ring with a cat's-eye stone from his finger. He tied a string around it and placed it around Angelina's neck. Her eyes grew bright. Travis smiled sadly, said goodbye to both mother and daughter, and quietly left the chapel.

William Travis

Alamo headquarters
March 5, 10:20 p.m.

Despite what he had told the men in their meeting, Travis still held out a shred of hope. He sat down to write one last letter. This one he addressed to the people of Goliad. Then he called for Jim Allen and gave him the letter to take to Fannin. He had chosen Allen not so much for his horsemanship as for his age. Allen was only 16 years old. If anyone deserved to live through the siege, Travis felt it was he. Even if Allen tried to come back, Travis was certain the battle would be over by then. Allen didn't seem to realize this. "I'll see you in a few days, Colonel," he said as he left the room.

"Of course," replied Travis. "God speed to you, Jim."

He went out to see Allen off and then made his final rounds of the sentries. Lastly, Travis checked on the three pickets in their hiding places just outside the fort. If the Mexicans should attack in the night, the pickets would sound the alarm. Then Travis returned to his rooms. Already there was a man named Joe, an enslaved person whom Travis kept with him in Texas. Joe was sound asleep, and Travis, too, tried to get a little sleep.

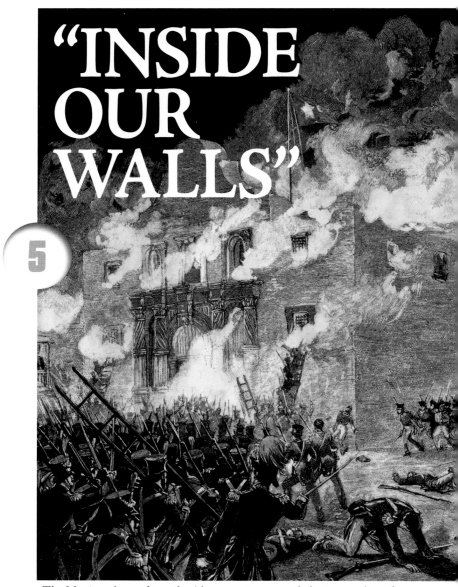

"INSIDE OUR WALLS"

5

The Mexicans' assault on the Alamo sent an overwhelming number of soldiers toward the fort.

Manuel Fernandez Castrillon

Outside north wall of the Alamo
March 6, 5 a.m.

General Castrillon held his breath in the chilled, dark air and waited. His troops were ready to attack. Some wielded muskets and bayonets. Others clutched ladders in their hands. There was no sign of Santa Anna. Their great leader was back at the earthworks waiting for the battle to begin. It did not surprise Castrillon that Santa Anna was not leading the charge. He was ready to sacrifice hundreds of men for his glory, but would not risk his own life. Yet the men loved him anyway, something Castrillon could not understand.

As if to prove this point, suddenly one of his soldiers cried, "Viva, Santa Anna!" Others joined in the cry. Before Castrillon knew it, they were running toward the Alamo. The battle was on. The general drew his sword and joined the attack.

William Travis

Travis was awakened from a restless sleep by John Baugh, the officer of the day. "Colonel Travis," Baugh cried, "the Mexicans are coming!"

Travis jumped out of bed, threw on his jacket, and seized his sword and shotgun. "Come on, Joe!" he yelled to his slave, sleeping nearby.

Together they ran after Baugh, and Travis cried words of encouragement to the men on the walls. Why hadn't the pickets warned them? It suddenly occurred to him that the Mexicans might have killed them before the attack. Now he could hear a terrible rumble. It was the sound of hundreds of Mexican soldiers running toward the fort. Travis hoisted himself up the wall to see them.

Joe

Joe stood and watched as his master fired his shotgun at the advancing Mexicans from atop the wall. A volley of bullets came in reply. Suddenly Travis fell back, his shotgun falling over the wall. He dropped down the bank and came to rest on the ground. Joe rushed to him. Blood was pouring out of a bullet wound in Travis's head. His eyes flickered for a moment and then became fixed in death. Joe shuddered. The commander of the Alamo was one of its first casualties.

Joe was too stunned to speak. He turned and fled to the barracks. He ran into a tiny storage room and shut the door behind him. He would remain hidden as long as possible. There was nothing else he could do.

Davy Crockett

The Mexicans were coming from every direction. Crockett and his sharpshooters held them back at this most vulnerable point of the fort. The soldiers rushed forward into the ditch below the walls and lifted their wooden ladders. They were sitting ducks

Inside the walls of the Alamo the Texians and Mexicans fought at close range.

for the riflemen. However, Crockett and his men made themselves easy targets by standing and firing down on them. As the riflemen moved back for safety, some soldiers clambered up the wall on their ladders. Crockett rushed back and pushed one ladder away. The soldiers on it toppled down, falling onto their comrades. Crockett grabbed another loaded rifle and fired down upon them.

Martin Perfecto de Cós

By the north wall of the Alamo
March 6, 5:35 a.m.

The general watched his men rush to the walls. They threw their ladders against the wall and climbed up. He saw one man after another drop, hit by the riflemen's bullets. Even worse, his soldiers in the rear were shooting their own comrades on the ladders as they fired upward. "Hold your fire!" he cried to the rear guard, but his voice was lost in the chaos of battle.

Susanna Dickinson

Dickinson could hear the cries and gunfire and knew the battle was underway. She looked down at Angelina, her little hands clinging tightly to her mother's apron. The sounds of the fighting were growing louder and louder. Then all at once, the chapel door burst open. In rushed 16-year-old Galba Fuqua, a Tejano. He stared at her wild-eyed and tried to speak but couldn't. To her horror she saw that he had been shot in the jaw and was holding it together with both hands. Unable to speak, he turned and rushed out.

A few moments later, the door opened again. It was Almeron! Her husband, bathed in sweat and blood, rushed to her side. "Good God, Sue!" he cried. "The Mexicans are inside our walls! If they spare you, save my child." Then he kissed her, hugged Angelina, and rushed out. She wondered if she would ever see him again.

Gregorio Esparza

Esparza kept firing his small cannon from inside the chapel directly below the high platform. Up there, Dickinson and the other artillery men fired the three 12-pound cannons at the advancing Mexicans outside the chapel. The Mexicans had gotten hold of the Texians' 18-pound cannon, turned it on the chapel, and began firing at Dickinson and his men. Esparza watched as one by one the brave men above on the platform fell dead. One man grabbed a child nearby and leaped to his death from the platform rather than be killed by enemy soldiers. Then the chapel doors broke open, and Mexican soldiers flooded in. Before Esparza could fire again, a soldier ran up and bayoneted him in the side. Another soldier shot him, and his world went dark.

Davy Crockett and his men had to defend a vulnerable position.

Martín Perfecto de Cós

The plaza
March 6, 6:00 a.m.

General Cós and what remained of his men were inside the fort. The battle no longer was fought with artillery and muskets. Now it was conducted with swords and bayonets and rifles swung as clubs. The Texians had nowhere to hide in the open plaza, although some made it alive to the barrack buildings. The soldiers rushed into the barracks rooms and stabbed and bayoneted every Texian they could find. Cós had had enough. He grabbed a passing bugler and told him to blow the signal for cease-fire. The bugler did so. But to the general's dismay the killing continued without pause.

Davy Crockett

The plaza
March 6, 6:05 a.m.

Surrounded by the enemy, Crockett had no time to reload or grab another rifle. He grabbed the barrel of his rifle and swung it at the attacking soldiers like a club. Down they fell as he struck their heads. Four. Five. Six. Then a seventh. But he didn't see the Mexican officer with his drawn sword until it was too late. The man swung and struck Crockett in the head just above his right eye. He fell to the hard earth and a dozen soldiers closed in on him with their bayonets.

A depiction of the death of Davy Crockett

Jim Bowie

His room near the chapel
March 6, 6:10 a.m.

Bowie wasn't afraid to die. But to die alone in this
airless room, helpless on his pallet, was not his wish.
He heard the soldiers growing closer and looked
down at the two loaded pistols next to him. He had
hoped to go out shooting, yet he lacked the strength
to even lift the pistols. Bowie could hear the tramp of
feet now just outside his door. He clenched his fists

and looked up. The door swung open and in burst a half dozen soldiers. They stared at him, surprised perhaps to see this sick man lying helpless before them. Bowie smiled as they rushed toward him. His only regret was that he wasn't standing.

Santa Anna

The Alamo
March 6, 6:30 a.m.

The general had watched the battle from the earthworks, the sky ablaze with cannon fire. Now, as he arrived on the scene, the Alamo was strangely quiet. The old mission had fallen and Santa Anna had come to claim his victory. It was all over in just 90 minutes. As he made the rounds of the plaza, Santa Anna passed many dead men, both Texians and Mexicans. There was no final body count yet, but he could see that many of his soldiers had died. It was the price of victory that Santa Anna was willing to pay. The important thing was that the rebels were dead and would serve as a bloody example to those traitors who remained.

Susanna Dickinson

The chapel that was once a sanctuary had become a killing ground. Only moments earlier, Dickinson had watched in horror as an Alamo gunner ran in, pursued by a group of enemy soldiers. They savagely bayoneted him to death, his cries still ringing in her ears. Then two boys, sons of another gunner, rushed in and were also stabbed to death. Would her turn be next? The soldiers ordered her to go to a small room near the Alamo's main entrance. She waited fearfully there with Angelina in her arms. Her heart leapt up when Mrs. Esparza and her children joined her.

As they hugged and wept for their men, an officer entered.

"Is Mrs. Dickinson here?" he asked.

Paralyzed by fear, she was unable to speak.

"Is Mrs. Dickinson here?" he repeated louder. "Speak out. It's a matter of life and death."

"Yes," she said.

The officer told her his name was Colonel Almonte. "If you want to save your life, follow me," he said.

She and Angelina followed him out of the chapel and into the plaza. She tried to avert her eyes from the bodies strewn on the ground. But out of the corner of her eye she saw a familiar figure in buckskin lying still on the ground. Next to him lay a coonskin cap. It was Colonel Crockett. She kept walking.

Joe

A room in the barracks
March 6, 6:40 a.m.

Joe sat in the small, dark room as the battle raged outside. Bullets had made holes in the door, and finding a gun, Joe fired back through one of the holes. But when the fighting died down, he put the gun down.

Then when all was quiet, he heard a voice call out in English, "Are there any Negroes here?"

There was no use in trying to hide any longer, he reasoned.

"Yes, here's one," he yelled back. Then he opened the door and stepped into the courtyard.

He immediately regretted his decision as two soldiers came at him. One grazed his side with a bayonet. The other fired his musket and hit him in the shoulder. But the wounds weren't serious. Before the soldiers could do him any further harm, the officer who had called out appeared. He told the soldiers to back off. He then escorted Joe to another room in the barracks. There he was brought before a tall, thin man, all dressed in black.

The man smiled at Joe and introduced himself. "I am General Santa Anna," he said.

Joe was stunned. The general assured him that no harm would come to him. He told Joe that Mexico had abolished slavery and that he would soon be free to leave. He asked Joe about the American forces and their numbers. Joe tried to answer as best he could. But he didn't want to say anything that would help lead to the capture of the other Texians.

"Now I have one more favor to ask you," Santa Anna said. "I would like you to identify the bodies of Travis, Crockett, and Jim Bowie."

Joe winced. He had seen his master die, and he had no desire to see his body now. He felt the same about Bowie and Crockett, both good men. But he knew it would be dangerous to say no to Santa Anna. So Joe agreed and was led out of the room by Santa Anna and several soldiers. In the courtyard the Alamo was beginning to fill up with the first light of dawn.

Manuel Fernandez Castrillon

The Alamo
March 6, 7:00 a.m.

The general had seen with his own eyes that the Alamo's defenders were all dead. He had seen more than he had wanted to see of the killing. His soldiers, Mexico's finest, had stabbed and shot men with a brutality that shocked him. But not all the Texians were dead. Soldiers were surrounding a group of six captives. They told Castrillon they had found them hiding in a back room.

"Shall we kill them, sir?" one soldier asked.

"No," replied Castrillon. "Leave them to me to handle."

He turned to the captive men. They looked at him with hollow eyes, filled with hopelessness.

"Come with me to the man in charge," the general told them, "and you will be saved."

There had been enough killing for one day. Surely even Santa Anna must see that. He would honor Castrillon's request to spare these men. He was sure of it.

Moments later he stepped into Santa Anna's temporary headquarters.

"Sir, here are six prisoners I have taken alive; how shall I dispose of them?" he asked.

Santa Anna looked briefly at the six captives and then turned back to Castrillon, his eyes glowing with fury.

"Have I not told you before how to dispose of them?" he said. "Why do you bring them to me?"

Santa Anna turned away sharply. As Santa Anna hurried past another group of soldiers, Castrillon heard him say, "Take them out and shoot them."

The officer in charge hesitated to carry out the orders. But several of Santa Anna's own guard were eager to please their commander. Without hesitation they drew their swords and rushed at the helpless prisoners. Castrillon barely escaped being run through himself. He cursed Santa Anna under his breath and fled from the bloody scene.

SANTA ANNA'S TRIUMPH

The battle and its aftermath left the Alamo in ruins.

Santa Anna

The general looked guardedly at Francisco Ruiz, the alcalde (mayor) of San Antonio. Ruiz had been a friend of the Texians and had been under house arrest during the siege. Santa Anna didn't trust him, but now he needed him.

"We have many dead soldiers," he told Ruiz. "I want you to see that their bodies are brought to the cemetery and properly buried."

"Very well, El Presidente," replied the mayor. "And what about the bodies of the Texians?"

"Traitors do not deserve to be buried," snapped the general. "Drag them out in the open air and burn them.

I will send my dragoons into the forest to bring wood for their pyre," Santa Anna said. "You will see to the rest."

Ruiz nodded.

"That is all," said the general, dismissing the mayor with a wave of his hand.

Sam Houston

Washington-on-the-Brazos
March 6, 3 p.m.

Sam Houston, newly appointed commander of the Texas Army, listened as Travis's letter was read on the convention floor. The letter was dated March 3. It was clear that the Alamo needed reinforcements and quickly. One delegate cried out that they should immediately ride to San Antonio to save the Alamo.

As the delegates argued over what to do, Sam Houston rose to his feet and called for silence.

"Yes, we should go to Travis's aid," he said. "But before you leave you must write a constitution. Without a plan of government we cannot expect to receive help from the United States and other countries. Without this help our cause is lost."

Most of the delegates agreed with Houston. They voted to stay and draw up a constitution. Satisfied, Houston left the hall with a few companions and rode south. His destination was Gonzales, where Major Neill was waiting with 300 volunteers. Then with a sizable force they would head for the Alamo.

Martin Perfecto de Cós

The Alamo
March 6, 4 p.m.

It had been a long and terrible day and General Cós wished it were over. He had accounted himself well in the battle and for that he was grateful. He was once again, it seemed, in the good graces of his brother-in-law Santa Anna—at least for the time being. As he gathered his thoughts, a soldier approached him.

"Sir, may I have a word with you?" the soldier asked.

Cós looked at the man's clean uniform. "You were not in the battle?" he asked.

"No," admitted the soldier. "I was at home in San Antonio. You see, my brother, Gregorio, was one of the men at the Alamo."

Cós did see. What man would want to fight against his own brother in battle?

"I would like, with your permission," continued Esparza, "to look for my brother's body and then take it to the cemetery for burial."

The general did not know what to say. Santa Anna had given the order to burn all the bodies of the rebels. On the other hand, he felt sorry for Esparza. His brother may have been on the wrong side, but he was still a Mexican.

"Very well," Cós said. "Go find your brother and bury him. And if anyone tries to stop you, tell them that General Cós gave you permission."

Francisco Esparza thanked him profusely. "Go quickly," Cós told him. "If you don't find him in time he will be burned with the others."

Esparza nodded and rushed off. Cós wondered if Santa Anna would be displeased with his decision. It was too late to worry about that now. He knew that he had done the right thing.

Fernandez Ruiz

Outside the Alamo
March 6, 5 p.m.

Ruiz's townsmen had done their work well. The pyre stood high against the bright blue sky. The wood and brush were in layers, and between each layer were the bodies of the Alamo dead. He gave a signal and a man set a torch to the bottom layer of wood. It crackled and snapped and soon orange flames rose into the air. As Ruiz watched black smoke rise from the pyre, one of his men came up to him.

"Have all the soldiers' bodies been brought to the cemetery?" Ruiz asked him.

"Yes, Alcalde," said the man, "but there is just one problem. There is not room in the cemetery to bury them all."

"Then bury as many as you can," replied Ruiz.

"And what of the others?" the man asked.

Ruiz looked up at the black smoke spiraling into the sky. He thought of the bodies burning, bodies of men he once knew and admired.

"Throw the rest of them into the river," he said.

The man nodded and ran off.

Santa Anna be damned, thought Ruiz.

Santa Anna

His San Antonio headquarters
March 6, 6 p.m.

The general had finished his inspection of the Alamo and had delivered a brief victory speech. Now there was just one task left to perform this day. He sat down at his desk to write an official report to the officials back in Mexico City.

Santa Anna showed little mercy in his victory.

"Victory belongs to the army, which at this moment . . . achieved a complete and glorious triumph that will render its memory imperishable," he wrote. Then he gave the count of the dead and wounded. He tripled the actual death toll of the rebels and greatly reduced the casualties on his own side. He saw nothing wrong in a little exaggeration. After all, there would be more and greater victories to come in the war against the Texians.

Susanna Dickinson

The stone house, San Antonio
March 7, 11 a.m.

Susanna Dickinson spent an unhappy night in the stone house. Angelina slept fitfully, but her mother remained awake nearly all night. All she could think about was the death of her husband and the other brave men of the Alamo. She would see none of them again. Not in this world. And what would become of her and her daughter, the only Texians left from the Alamo?

One by one, the Mexican women and their children were led from the stone house to be interviewed by Santa Anna. Finally it was her turn. Colonel Almonte escorted her and Angelina across the plaza to Santa Anna's headquarters.

The general greeted her with a smile. He seemed to be particularly taken with Angelina. He began to talk in Spanish. When he finished his speech Almonte translated his words into English. "The general would like to take you and your daughter to Mexico City with him," he said.

Dickinson was stunned. "Never," she whispered to the colonel.

"Let me finish," Almonte said. "The general would like to adopt your daughter and see that she is raised properly with a good education."

Dickinson was not impressed. "Tell him that I cannot accept his offer and that we cannot go with him."

The colonel spoke in Spanish with Santa Anna, whose expression turned less friendly. "The general will make his decision about your future soon," Almonte told her. "In the meantime, you will remain at the stone house."

Dickinson looked at him, her eyes pleading.

"Please don't let him do this. You must convince him to let us go. Please."

Almonte patted her hand gently. "I will do what I can," he said.

Joe

San Antonio
March 11, 10:20 a.m.

Joe thought about the last four days since the Alamo's fall with mixed feelings. He was grateful to be alive and not in prison. On the other hand, he felt guilty and slightly ashamed that he had given Santa Anna information about the Texian forces. He didn't think that he had given the general anything important, but he had remained his willing guest. Santa Anna had not said Joe had to stay at San Antonio, but he did not say he could leave either. After three days, Joe decided he'd had enough of the place and memories of the Alamo's fall. He packed a few belongings and headed out on the road to Gonzales. No one saw him leave. He had no desire to return to being a slave, but he'd rather be with the Texians than remain here. He didn't want to be in the company of the soldiers who had killed so many inside the Alamo, some of whom he considered friends.

Susanna Dickinson

The stone house, San Antonio
March 11, noon

The four days since Dickinson's interview with Santa Anna had been hard. No word came about what her future would be. She tried to be brave for Angelina, but the child sensed something was wrong.

Suddenly there was a rap at the door. It was Colonel Almonte. He was smiling, a good sign. "The general has agreed to let you return to your people," he told her. "You will leave at once. My servant Ben will accompany you."

Dickinson thanked him profusely. Ben, a young Mexican, was waiting for them in the plaza with a pony and a mule. He had a blanket for her and food for the journey ahead. Together they left the plaza and rode past the Alamo on the road to Gonzales. Near the fort that had been her home for weeks, she saw a smoldering pile of burnt wood. She turned away, not wanting to look another second at the pyre. She knew there lay the remains of her husband and the other brave men of the Alamo.

Joe

Along the Salado River
4 miles (6 km) east of San Antonio
March 11, 1:30 p.m.

Joe was resting in the shade of a tree when he heard the whinny of a horse. He peered out and saw a woman and child on a pony and a Mexican walking beside a mule. He recognized Dickinson at once and his heart beat fast. Now he would have company on his journey to Gonzales. He ran out and waved his arms. Susanna Dickinson seemed pleased to see him, the Mexican less so. He wanted to talk about the men who died, but decided this was the wrong moment to do so. After a few minutes, they fell into line and continued down the dusty road to Gonzales. Joe carried Angelina on his shoulders.

Sam Houston

It had been a long, hard ride from Washington-on-the-Brazos, and Sam Houston was ready for a rest. But before he could take off his boots, men came announcing that two Tejanos had arrived and had news from the Alamo. The general had them brought to him at once. They told him that the Alamo had been taken and all the defenders were dead. It was news that Houston and his 100 men did not want to believe. Suspicious of the men, he had them arrested and held in the jail. Houston tried to prevent the news from spreading, but it quickly did. At least a dozen women in Gonzales had husbands at the Alamo. The night air filled with their shrieks and cries. Houston was angry, both with Santa Anna and with himself for not taking action sooner. He sat down and dashed off a letter to Colonel Fannin at Goliad. His message was short and direct. He ordered Fannin to blow up the presidio, abandon Goliad, and head north. If the Alamo had indeed fallen, he didn't want to lose another remote fort to the enemy. The Texian forces had to remain united and on the move.

Susanna Dickinson

On the road to Gonzales
March 13, noon

The small party was only miles from Gonzales when Dickinson saw riders in the distance. Three horsemen were approaching fast. Joe turned to Mrs. Dickinson. "They could be Comanches," he said. "We've got to hide."

"No," she replied firmly. "I will not hide. If they are Indians, I will face them. I won't run, Joe. I'm tired of running."

Joe pleaded with her, but she refused to hide. The horsemen were not Comanches. They were scouts for Sam Houston. They listened intently to Dickinson's tale of woe.

"General Houston needs to hear this at once," said Deaf Smith, the head scout. "We'll take you to him." But knowing their party would be moving slowly, Smith sent one of the other scouts on ahead to spread the sad news.

Sam Houston heard about the fall of the Alamo days later.

Sam Houston

Gonzales
March 13, 4:15 p.m.

Tears came to Sam Houston's eyes as he held Susanna Dickinson's hand and listened to her describe the fall of the Alamo. The story of the two Tejanos had been confirmed. Travis, Bowie, Crockett . . . they were all dead. There was only one course left to Houston. It was to retreat and draw Santa Anna to him for a fight. It was a fight Houston was determined to win. He rallied all his troops, numbering 374 men, and by late evening was ready to move. The townspeople of Gonzales and the Dickinson party followed them.

"What should we do with the town, general?" one of Houston's officers asked.

"Burn it to the ground," replied Houston. "We'll leave nothing behind that Santa Anna can use." Then he gave the order to move out.

EPILOGUE

After retreating from Santa Anna's army for weeks, Sam Houston launched a surprise attack on April 21, 1836. The Texians cried, "Remember the Alamo!" as they charged Santa Anna's troops near the San Jacinto River. The battle lasted only 18 minutes. The Mexicans were completely defeated. Santa Anna himself was captured the following day and only released after promising Texas its independence.

Texas became an independent republic and elected Sam Houston as its first president. Independence, unfortunately, did not extend to enslaved African Americans. The new republic legalized slavery in its constitution. Slave labor became important to the cotton industry in East Texas. President Houston disliked slavery, but did not openly oppose it and was himself a slaveholder. Nearly 10 years later, on December 29, 1845, Texas was admitted to the United States as the 28th state. Today the Alamo is a revered historical site and is visited by 2.5 million people each year.

Many descendants of men who died at the Alamo carried on their names proudly. James Bowie's brother Rezin, upon hearing of his death, left for Texas. He served as a colonel in the Texas Army. Davy Crockett's son Robert also traveled to Texas and became a lieutenant in the Texan cavalry. Crockett's oldest son, John Wesley, ran for his father's seat in Congress in 1837 and served for two terms. Less happy was the story of William

The Texians avenged the defeat at the Alamo with a crushing victory at the Battle of San Jacinto in 1836.

Travis's son Charles. He grew up to become a U.S. Army officer in Texas but was court-martialed. The charges against him included cheating at cards and leaving camp without permission. Charles Travis was convicted and dismissed from service in 1856. He fought unsuccessfully to clear his name and died of a lung disease called consumption (tuberculosis) at his sister Susan's home in 1860. Susan Travis died eight years later.

Gregorio Esparza's son Enrique survived the siege with his mother and became a farmer in San Antonio. He married and had seven children. Enrique was interviewed about the Alamo in 1907. "It is burned into my brain and indelibly seared there," he said. "Neither age nor infirmity could make me forget, for the scene was one of such horror that it could never be forgotten." He died on December 20, 1917, the last survivor of the Alamo.

John Sutherland returned after the Alamo's fall with reinforcements. He later moved to Cibolo Creek, 20 miles (32 km) east of San Antonio. He cared for cholera patients and other sick people who visited the sulfur springs near his home. His home became the center of a new community, Sutherland Springs. He served as justice of the peace and a school board member. Sutherland wrote a book, *The Fall of the Alamo*, in 1860 that was finally published more than a century later. He died on April 11, 1867.

Susanna Dickinson settled in Houston, a new town named for the hero of San Jacinto. She married four more times, only finding happiness again with her fifth husband, a German-born cabinetmaker. She was interviewed many times about the Alamo, often telling conflicting stories. She died in 1883 at age 68. Her daughter, Angelina, married twice and had four children. She abandoned them to lead a wandering life and died at age 34 of illness.

Joe, Travis's slave, eventually returned to his owner's estate near Columbia, South Carolina. On April 21, 1837, Joe ran away, aided by a Mexican man. A $50 reward was put on his head, but he was never captured. He was last reported living as a freed man, possibly in Alabama, in 1875.

Louis Rose managed to reach a friend's house after leaving the Alamo. He suffered serious leg wounds from cactuses he had to walk through in his escape. He opened a meat market for a time, but his reputation as the "coward of the Alamo" hurt his business. He finally was taken in at a Louisiana plantation where he died of his old injuries in 1850.

Colonel James Fannin, the man who refused to come to the Alamo's aid, finally left Goliad on Houston's orders. He was attacked by Mexican troops at the Battle of Coleto Creek. Fannin surrendered, and his captured troops were massacred by the Mexicans on Palm Sunday, March 27, 1836. Fannin himself was the last to die, executed by a firing squad.

Sam Houston was elected one of Texas's first U.S. senators when it became part of the United States. He later served as Texas's governor in the years before the outbreak of the Civil War. Houston refused to endorse Texas's secession from the United States to become part of the Confederacy. For this he was removed from office. Sam Houston was denounced by his friends and even his own children. He died in bed on July 26, 1863, in the midst of the war he so strongly opposed. His last words to his wife Margaret were, "Texas, Margaret, Texas."

Santa Anna outlived his old adversary, Sam Houston. He was in and out of power in Mexico from 1838 until the outbreak of the U.S.-Mexican War in 1846. That war ended in defeat for Mexico. The country lost much of its territory in the southwest, including the future states of Arizona and New Mexico. In exile in Cuba, Santa Anna's schemes to return to power failed. He finally settled in the Bahamas in 1870, where he wrote his life story, greatly exaggerating his achievements. He died in 1876.

Santa Anna's brother-in-law, Martin Perfecto de Cós, was also taken captive after the Battle of San Jacinto. He later was put in command of an outpost in Tuxpan, Mexico. He served there until his death in 1854. Manuel Fernandez Castrillon was also present at San Jacinto. He was shaving in his tent when the Texians attacked. His men implored him to flee for his life, but Castrillon refused to run. Even Texian officers tried to save his life. He was shot to death by Texian soldiers out to avenge the Alamo. It was ironic that they killed an officer who had tried to save Texian lives at the Alamo.

TIMELINE

DECEMBER 10, 1835 Texian forces defeat Mexican troops led by General Martin Perfecto de Cós, drive them from the Alamo, and take over San Antonio de Bexar.

JANUARY 19, 1836 Colonel Jim Bowie arrives at the Alamo with orders to destroy it, but decides that it is defendable.

JANUARY 25, 1836 General Santa Anna leaves Saltillo, Mexico, with a large army on a 465-mile (748-km) march north to San Antonio to crush the Texian rebels.

FEBRUARY 23, 1836 Santa Anna's army arrives in San Antonio and the Texians and Tejanos make their stand in the Alamo.

FEBRUARY 24, 1836 Jim Bowie, ill with a mysterious disease, turns over complete command of the Alamo to Colonel William Travis.

FEBRUARY 26–27, 1836 Colonel James Fannin starts from Goliad with 450 men to aid the Alamo. However, meager supplies, broken wagon wheels, and dissenting volunteers soon make him decide to abandon the mission.

FEBRUARY 28, 1836 Santa Anna orders an intensive artillery attack on the Alamo while waiting for more troops to arrive.

MARCH 1, 1836 John Smith arrives at the Alamo with 32 reinforcements from Gonzales.

MARCH 2, 1836 At a convention in Washington-on-the-Brazos, Texian delegates issue a declaration of independence from Mexico.

MARCH 3, 1836 Some 1,100 Mexican reinforcements arrive at San Antonio. Travis receives news of more reinforcements coming to the Alamo's aid.

MARCH 4, 1836 Santa Anna meets with his officers to determine a time for a full-out assault, but no final decision is made.

MARCH 5, 1836 Travis asks the men of the Alamo to decide whether to leave or stay and fight; only one man, Louis Rose, chooses to leave.

MARCH 6, 1836, 5 A.M. The Mexicans make a final assault on the Alamo. Within 90 minutes they have taken the fort and all the male defenders are killed in the fighting.

MARCH 6, 1836, 3 P.M. The delegates at the Texas convention agree to draw up a constitution for their new republic. Sam Houston leaves for Gonzales to collect volunteers to go to the Alamo, not knowing the battle is over.

MARCH 6, 1836, 5 P.M. The Alamo dead are burned on a wooden pyre outside the fort.

MARCH 11, 1836 Susanna Dickinson and her daughter, the only Texian survivors of the Alamo, are released by Santa Anna and journey to Gonzales with Joe, an enslaved man who also escaped the Alamo with his life.

MARCH 13, 1836 Dickinson and her party arrive in Gonzales and tell Sam Houston the tragic story of the Alamo's fall.

APRIL 21, 1836 Houston's army surprises Santa Anna's forces at the Battle of San Jacinto and defeat them soundly. Santa Anna is captured and agrees to allow Texas to be independent in exchange for his freedom.

DECEMBER 29, 1845 After nearly 10 years as an independent republic, Texas becomes the 28th state of the United States.

DECEMBER 20, 1917 Enrique Esparza, the last living survivor of the Alamo, dies.

GLOSSARY

alcalde (al-KAL-de)—a mayor in Mexico, Spain, and the early southwestern United States

artillery (ar-TIL-uh-ree)—mounted guns, such as cannons, that launch cannonballs and other projectiles

barracks (BAR-uhks)—a group of buildings where soldiers are lodged in a fort

batteries (BAT-uh-rees)—two or more pieces of artillery, large guns, used in combined action in warfare

casualty (KAZH-oo-uhl-tee)—a soldier who is removed from action by being killed, wounded, or made sick

cholera (KOL-uhr-uhn)—a contagious disease marked by diarrhea and dehydration

constitution (KON-sti-TOO-shuhn)—a document defining a country or state's system of government and laws

court-martialed (KORT-MAR-shuhled)—put on trial in a military court on charges of breaking military law

dragoons (dra-GOONS)—infantry soldiers on horseback

earthwork (URTH-work)—a military construction made of earth to protect soldiers from enemy fire

empresario (EM-pruh-SA-ri-o)—a person who brought settlers to Texas in exchange for grants of land from Mexico

litter (LIT-uhr)—a stretcher for carrying a sick or wounded person

packet (PAK-it)—a small package or parcel

palisade (PAL-uh-sad)—a fence of stakes or poles set up as an enclosure for defense; a primitive kind of fort

pallet (PAL it)—a makeshift bed often with a straw-filled mattress

parapets (PAR-uh-pits)—the outer, low protective walls of a fort

pickets (PIK its)—soldiers placed outside a fort or line of defense to warn against an enemy attack

plaza (PLA-zuh)—a public square in a city or town

pyre (PIER)—a pile of wood for burning dead bodies

quarantining (KOWR-uhn-teen-ing)—isolating people with a contagious disease to prevent it from spreading to others

siege (SEJ)—a prolonged attack on a fort or city to get the defenders to surrender

Tejanos (ta-HA-nos)—Mexicans who sided against the Mexican government and supported Texas independence

Texians (TEX-ee-ans)—settlers from the United States and elsewhere who supported Texas independence from Mexico

CRITICAL THINKING QUESTIONS

1. The Battle of the Alamo was, on the surface, a minor battle in the history of warfare. Why has it taken on such historical importance in Texan and American history?

2. What actions, or lack of action, contributed to the downfall of the Alamo? What role did the slow spreading of news and messages by horse and rider play in the tragedy?

3. We tend to see wars from the perspective of our own side and make the enemy out to be bad people. What actions of Mexicans—both Tejanos and soldiers in Santa Anna's army—disprove this theory?

INTERNET SITES

Use FactHound to find Internet sites related to this book.

Visit *www.facthound.com*

Just type in 9781543541984 and go.

FURTHER READING

Gunderson, Jessica. *The Alamo: Myths, Legends and Facts*. North Mankato, MN: Capstone Press, 2015.

Kerr, Rita. *Girl of the Alamo: The Story of Susanna Dickinson*. Fort Worth, TX: Eakin Press, 2016.

Walker, Paul Robert. *Remember the Alamo: Texians, Tejanos, and Mexicans Tell Their Stories*. Washington, D.C.: National Geographic Children's Books, 2015.

SELECTED BIBLIOGRAPHY

Donovan, James. *The Blood of Heroes: The 13-Day Struggle for the Alamo and the Sacrifice That Forged a Nation*. Boston: Little Brown, 2012.

Hoyt, Edwin P. *The Alamo: An Illustrated History*. Dallas, TX: Taylor Publishing Company, 1999.

Lord, Walter. *A Time to Stand: The Epic of the Alamo Seen as a Great National Experience*. New York: Harper Brothers, 1961.

Ramsdell, Charles. "The Storming of the Alamo." *American Heritage*, February 1961, 30–33, 90–93.

INDEX

ABOUT THE AUTHOR

Steven Otfinoski has written more than 200 books for young readers. His previous books in the Tangled History series include *Day of Infamy: Attack on Pearl Harbor* and *Smooth Seas and a Fighting Chance: The Story of the Sinking of Titanic*. Among his many other books for Capstone are the You Choose book *World War II Infantrymen* and *The Split History of the Battle of Fort Sumter*. Three of his nonfiction books have been named Books for the Teen Age by the New York Public Library. He lives in Connecticut with his wife and dog.